The Master Key BLUEPRINT

The Master Key BLUEPRINT

Stacey M. Oliver

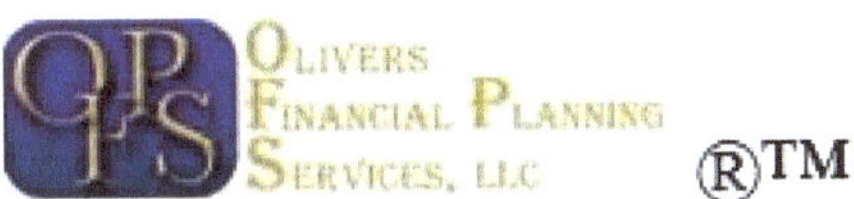

®TM

South Carolina

For more resources, please visit https://www.ofpsagency.com

Disclaimer

The advice contained in this guide may not be suitable for everyone. The author obtained information from sources that may be reliable and from her own experience. The information in this guide is provided for education and informational purposes only, without any express or implied warranty of any kind, including warranties of accuracy, completeness for any particular purpose. The material contained in this guide is not intended to be and does not constitute financial, legal or any other advice. The information is general in nature and is not specific to you the user or anyone else. The author, distributor and publisher particularly disclaims any liability, loss or risk taken by individuals who directly or indirectly act on the information contained herein. All readers must accept all and full responsibilities for their use of this material. All pictures used in this guide are for illustrated purposes only. The pictures are only licensed for use of this guide and must not be used for any other purpose without prior written permission of the rights holder.

Copyrights

OFPS, LLC Publishing

Work Cited

(https://en.oxforddictionaries.com/, n.d.)
(https://en.wikipedia.org/wiki/, n.d.)
(https://www.merriam-webster.com/, since 1828)
(https://www.investopedia.com/ask/answers/040715/how-does-your-checking-account-affect-your-credit-score.asp)
(https://www.creditkarma.com/article/CreditCardUtilizationAndScore)
(https://www.discover.com/free-credit-score)
(https://www.annualcreditreport.com/yourRights.action, since 2017)

Printed and Published in the United States of America

The Master Key BLUEPRINT
STACEY M. OLIVER

ISBN-13: 978-1-7350929-0-4

Interior Designs by STACEY M. OLIVER

A New Kind of Agency

Olivers Financial Planning Services, LLC

(aka OFPS, LLC) was incorporated and founded by Stacey M. Oliver, CEO, in 2015. Our mission is to create, enlighten, and empower committed effective stewards of finances. Our primary objective is to increase our clients' financial literacy awareness so they can fully understand how money works.

"Money can work hard for you instead of you working hard for it. Once that concept is learned then the vicious cycle and hold of debt can be removed."

For more resources, please visit https://www.ofpsagency.com

Hello

Hi, I'm ***Stacey M. Oliver***, your Barrier Breaker and Financial Locksmith.

I empower individuals with the <u>Master Key</u> to unlocking doors to complete financial freedom.

Now let me ask...What is keeping the doors locked to you obtaining total financial freedom? The answer is simple, *Barrier(s).* A barrier is an obstacle that prevents movement, access, or progress.

If you do not become empowered with the Master Key to complete financial freedom the trend of financial barriers and financial ignorance will continue to filter and recycle through you and/or your family.

If the financial barrier is not broken and destroyed in our lives, there will not be a financial legacy left for our next generation. Stop allowing the doors to remain locked to your financial freedom. **Possess the Master Key and start taking charge of unlocking doors to your financial wealth so you can begin to experience Financial FREEDOM.**

The Master Key Blueprint workbook will increase your financial knowledge base. Topics include Net Worth, Credit and Budgeting. This guide is a key success to your complete financial freedom.

The **Blueprint** breaks down how to become an effective money manager. The issue is most people are never taught how to manage their money once they start the work force. This workbook will educate you in simple terms how to maximize and manage the money you earn. It doesn't matter if you are in high school, just starting college or you have been in the work force for several years.

The **Blueprint** will teach you step by step how to strategize and plan everything, from setting, starting and sticking to a budget to establishing and maintaining good credit. Use this guide to construct your financial decisions, change your financial behavior and enjoy living the life of complete financial freedom.

OFPS

Table of Contents

RATE YOURSELF & SHIFT YOUR FOCUS

"Empowering Individuals with the Master Key to Complete Financial Freedom" -Stacey M. Oliver

Rate Yourself

Circle one for each category with five being strongly agree
and one being strongly disagree.

Determined 1 2 3 4 5

(firm decision; adamant; unwavering)

Self-motivated 1 2 3 4 5

(without supervision; initiative to undertake)

Self-discipline 1 2 3 4 5

(overcome one's weaknesses; the ability to make yourself do things that should be done)

Self-control 1 2 3 4 5

(the ability to manage your actions, feelings, and emotions)

Persistent 1 2 3 4 5

(continuing firmly in a course of action in spite of difficulty/opposition; continuing to endure over a prolonged period; preserving; lasting; enduring)

Shift Your Focus

Change your Focus from Poor to Rich.

"Change Your Mindset, Change Your Money."

It's all about *Eradicating* the negativity you have in your mind and *Affirm* it with a **YES**!!!

Shift Your Focus *continued...*

Declare what you will <u>Stop</u> and <u>Start</u> Today!

(Fill in the boxes under the START column.)

"Financial Freedom is a Language."

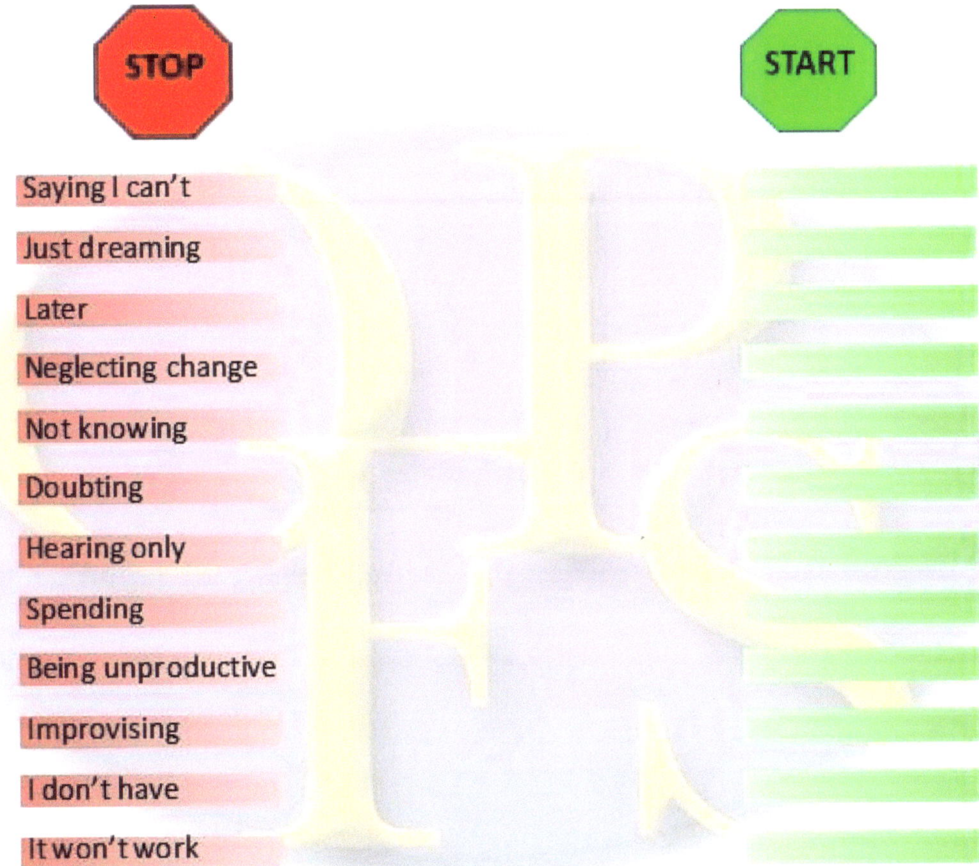

It's all about ***Eradicating*** the negativity you have in your mind and ***Affirm*** it with a **YES**!!!

Quick Reminders

Action Plan

FINANCIAL GOALS

"Excellence is not an act. Excellence is a habit. Excellence is what you habitually DO."

-Stacey M. Oliver

Becoming Financially Fit

- Do you know your net worth?
- What percentage of your income goes to retirement?
- Do you have a WILL?
- Do you have 3 – 6 months of living income stashed?
- Is your family protected?
- Do you know your credit score?
- Have you obtained and reviewed your credit report lately?
- Do you have emergency funds?
- Do you have or maintain a budget system?
- Do you find yourself spending more than you make?

GOALS

Growing your money with an open mind and exploring alternatives for long-term savings.

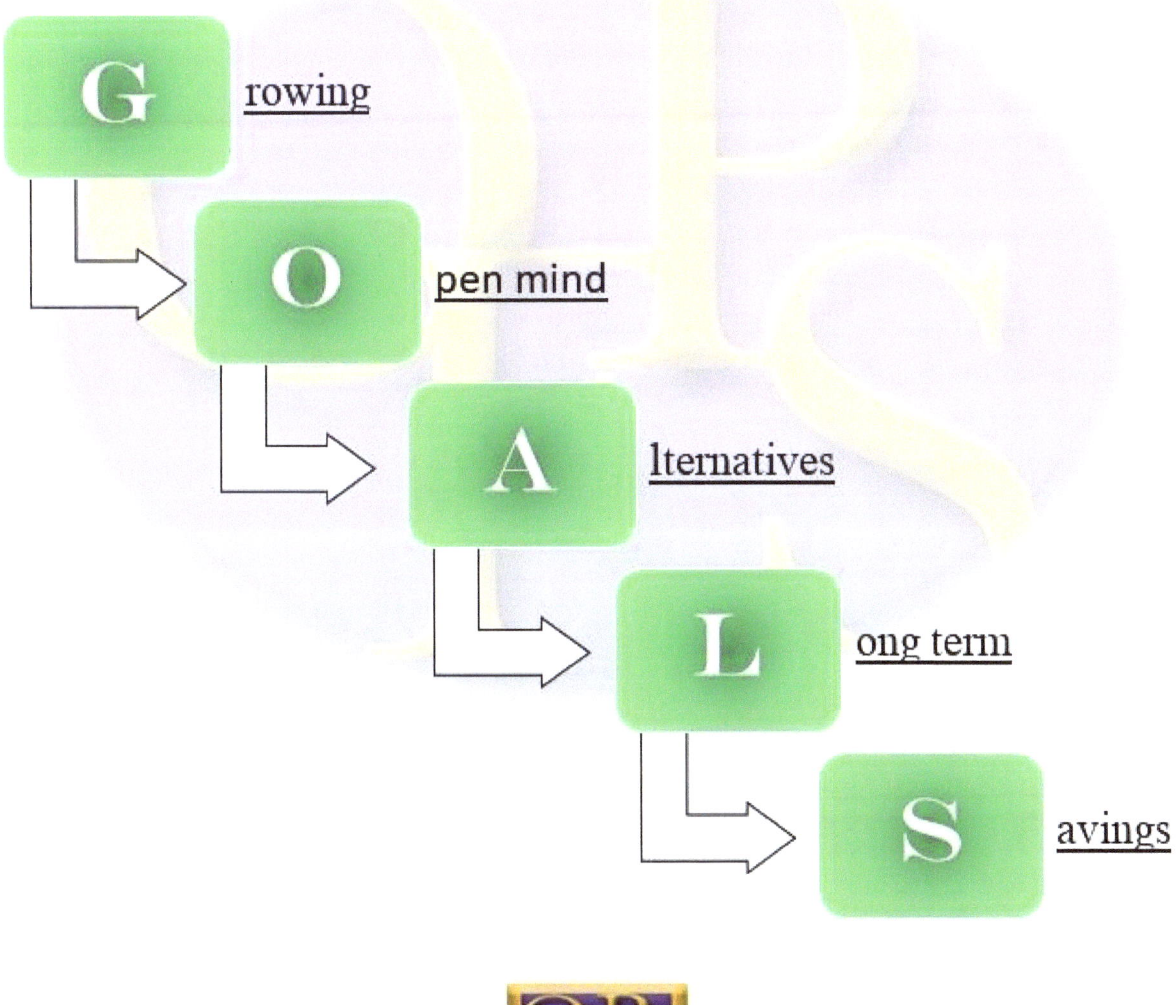

Financial Goals

- Brainstorm and picture your next 12 months or perhaps the next 10 years. Are you on the right track to meeting your financial goals or do you need to reset and make some changes?
- Determine an Outcome. Do you need to payoff some debt or pay down some debt? Do you need to increase your savings? Do you need to curtail your spending?
- Compose an attainable goal to payoff debt/pay down and/or increase savings.
- Analyze your goal and make sure it makes sense and it is attainable.
  a) The length of time it will take to meet goal.
  b) The cost factor (*the total amount of money needed*).
- Track your progress. Are you on your way to meeting goal?
- Keep going and complete your goal.
- Celebrate each milestone. Rather focusing on how much longer or how much more…focus on the outcome and the progress. Every minor step gets you to the major step. Focusing on the outcome keeps you motivated.
- Once goal is met, mark accomplishment.

Timeline worksheets have been provided to track your goals.

Financial Goals Timeline

Timeline

Brainstorm → Determine Outcome → Compose a Goal → Analyze Goal → Track Goal → Complete Goal → Conclude w/date of Completion

	Complete By MM/DD/YYYY	Action Plan
☐		
☐		
☐		
☐		
☐		
☐		
☐		
☐		
☐		
☐		

Financial Goals Timeline

Timeline

Brainstorm → Determine Outcome → Compose a Goal → Analyze Goal → Track Goal → Complete Goal → Conclude w/date of Completion

	Complete By MM/DD/YYYY	Action Plan
☐		
☐		
☐		
☐		
☐		
☐		
☐		
☐		
☐		
☐		

Financial Goals Timeline

Timeline

Brainstorm → Determine Outcome → Compose a Goal → Analyze Goal → Track Goal → Complete Goal → Conclude w/date of Completion

	Complete By MM/DD/YYYY	Action Plan
☐		
☐		
☐		
☐		
☐		
☐		
☐		
☐		
☐		
☐		

Financial Goals Timeline

Timeline

Brainstorm → Determine Outcome → Compose a Goal → Analyze Goal → Track Goal → Complete Goal → Conclude w/date of Completion

	Complete By MM/DD/YYYY	Action Plan
☐		
☐		
☐		
☐		
☐		
☐		
☐		
☐		
☐		
☐		

Quick Reminders

OFPS

NET WORTH

"Are you ready to make the decision to change your financial status? Complete financial freedom is attainable." -Stacey M. Oliver

Net Worth

Knowing your **Net Worth** is a simple equation:

ASSETS — LIABILITIES = NET WORTH

Net worth represents the properties owned, less any debt an individual has.

Net Worth

Net Worth

What is your current life cash value?

If you have more assets (own) than liabilities (owe), you have a positive net worth. If you do not, you have a negative net worth in other words no monetary cash value.

Assets/Own – Liab./Owe

= Net Worth

Bad	Good
Debt > Income	Debt < Income
Expenses > Income	Expenses < Income
Assets < Liabilities	Assets > Liabilities

>

Greater than

or

<

Less than

Net Worth

If your out of pocket expenses are more than your take home pay, here are some options to consider:

Set, Start and Stick to Budget

Eliminate Unnecessary Debt

Debt Consolidation

Refinance

"Money wasted is Money not well spent."

Test Your Knowledge

Net Worth is an individual's total assets of what's owned minus total liabilities or expenses of what's owed.

- ❑ True
- ❑ False

Net Worth

Calculate your **Net Worth** by completing the worksheet on the next few pages. A sample sheet has been provided for your guidance.

Extra worksheets have been provided to recalculate your net worth as you payoff debt and increase your assets, cash savings and/or investments.

NET WORTH

DATE: MM/DD/YYYY

ASSETS (OWN)		LIABILITIES (OWE)	
Personal Items	Estimated Value	Outstanding Debt/Loan Balances	Estimated Value
Home	205,000	Mortgage	150,000
Vacation Home		2nd Mortgage (Home Equity)	
Real Estate Property		Real Estate	
Automobiles	1,100	Automobiles	58,321
Motor Home		Student Loan	85,200
Boats		Finance Companies	6,609
Jewelry		Other Loans	
Fur			
Furniture		Other Debt	
Electronics		Credit Card Debt	10,200
Antiques	17,050	Other Debt	
Live Stocks			
Other Assts			
Cash or Equivalent to Cash			
Checking	400		
Savings	3,180		
CD's	500		
Money Market			
Life Insurance w/Cash Value (excluding Term)			
Other			
Investments			
Retirement (401K, IRA, Traditional IRS)	215,640		
Bonds			
Mutual Funds			
Individual Stock Shares			
Real Estate Property ((excluding Home)			
Other			
Total Assets	$442,870	Total LIABILITIES	$310,330
Estimated Net Worth:	$132,540		

SAMPLE

"Is your mindset serving as a barrier against your absolute economic power." – **Stacey M. Oliver**

NET WORTH

DATE:____

ASSETS (OWN)		LIABILITIES (OWE)	
Personal Items	Estimated Value	Outstanding Debt/Loan Balances	Estimated Value
Home		Mortgage	
Vacation Home		2nd Mortgage (Home Equity)	
Real Estate Property		Real Estate	
Automobiles		Automobiles	
Motor Home		Student Loan	
Boats		Finance Companies	
Jewelry		Other Loans	
Fur			
Furniture		Other Debt	
Electronics		Credit Card Debt	
Antiques		Other Debt	
Live Stocks			
Other Assts			
Cash or Equivalent to Cash			
Checking			
Savings			
CD's			
Money Market			
Life Insurance w/Cash Value (excluding Term)			
Other			
Investments			
Retirement (401K, IRA, Traditional IRS)			
Bonds			
Mutual Funds			
Individual Stock Shares			
Real Estate Property ((excluding Home)			
Other			
Total Assets	$	Total LIABILITIES	$
Estimated Net Worth: $			

"Is your mindset serving as a barrier against your absolute economic power." – **Stacey M. Oliver**

NET WORTH

DATE:______________________________

ASSETS (OWN)		LIABILITIES (OWE)	
Personal Items	Estimated Value	Outstanding Debt/Loan Balances	Estimated Value
Home		Mortgage	
Vacation Home		2nd Mortgage (Home Equity)	
Real Estate Property		Real Estate	
Automobiles		Automobiles	
Motor Home		Student Loan	
Boats		Finance Companies	
Jewelry		Other Loans	
Fur			
Furniture		Other Debt	
Electronics		Credit Card Debt	
Antiques		Other Debt	
Live Stocks			
Other Assts			
Cash or Equivalent to Cash			
Checking			
Savings			
CD's			
Money Market			
Life Insurance w/Cash Value (excluding Term)			
Other			
Investments			
Retirement (401K, IRA, Traditional IRS)			
Bonds			
Mutual Funds			
Individual Stock Shares			
Real Estate Property ((excluding Home)			
Other			
Total Assets	$	Total LIABILITIES	$
Estimated Net Worth: $			

"Is your mindset serving as a barrier against your absolute economic power." – **Stacey M. Oliver**

NET WORTH

DATE:______________________________

ASSETS (OWN)		LIABILITIES (OWE)	
Personal Items	Estimated Value	Outstanding Debt/Loan Balances	Estimated Value
Home		Mortgage	
Vacation Home		2nd Mortgage (Home Equity)	
Real Estate Property		Real Estate	
Automobiles		Automobiles	
Motor Home		Student Loan	
Boats		Finance Companies	
Jewelry		Other Loans	
Fur			
Furniture		Other Debt	
Electronics		Credit Card Debt	
Antiques		Other Debt	
Live Stocks			
Other Assts			
Cash or Equivalent to Cash			
Checking			
Savings			
CD's			
Money Market			
Life Insurance w/Cash Value (excluding Term)			
Other			
Investments			
Retirement (401K, IRA, Traditional IRS)			
Bonds			
Mutual Funds			
Individual Stock Shares			
Real Estate Property ((excluding Home)			
Other			
Total Assets	$	Total LIABILITIES	$
Estimated Net Worth: $			

"Is your mindset serving as a barrier against your absolute economic power." – **Stacey M. Oliver**

At-A-Glance

OFPS

CREDIT

"Knowledge, The Master Key to Financial Freedom."

-Stacey M. Oliver

Credit

Strong credit opens various gateways for the duration of regular day to day existence. You need your future to be better than your past…CHANGE. Why not choose the decision to change your present credit standing? Be certain your credit reflects positive change.

Constantly improving your credit is a lifestyle and a continued process. You may agree that it is very easy to fall in one of these categories:

Bad Credit	• Mismanaging Money • Forfeiting/Neglecting Obligations
No Credit	• No Existing Credit Established • Non-Sufficient Amount of Credit History
Over Extended Credit	• Too Many Credit Obligations • Amount of Credit too Large to Pay

How to Build Credit

The High Fives to Building Credit

- Secure credit cards is one way to establish credit.
- Become an authorized user for an existing responsible cardholder. Ensure activity is being reported to ALL three credit agencies.
- Utilize a major credit card for normal regular expenditures, such as; gas, utilities, groceries, etc. and payoff current balance.
- Do NOT become greater than 30 days delinquent on any credit reporting accounts.
- Take advantage of a Credit Builder Program.

Credit FICO Score Model

FICO Score is a registered trademark of the Fair Isaac Corporation in United States and other countries.

Note: TransUnion uses the FICO score model.

750-UP
Very Good

650-749
Good

550-649
Fair

300
Poor

- Experian is typically the lowest score.
- Transunion is typically the middle score.
- Equifax is typically the highest score.

FICO Credit Score

Key Pointers

- Establishing a good credit mixture such as installment loans and revolving credit influences 10% of your FICO Score. *(For example; car loan, credit card/line of credit, student loan, mortgage, etc.)*
- Length of Credit, also known as Aged Accounts, impacts 15% of FICO Score. *(Note: When disputing items reflecting negatively on credit report, the dispute may cause the clock to start over for the length of time the items will remain on report. For example; if a collection item is due to fall off the credit report within six months and a dispute is filed within the six months, the item will not fall off as scheduled but it will remain another 7 years from the date of the dispute.)*
- Inquiries make up 10% of your FICO Score.
- Revolving Utilization effects 30% of your FICO Score. *(Note: Simply keep all credit card balances below the 30% ratio or less of the credit card limit to ensure the utilization ratio is being maintained.)*
- On-time payments impact 35% of your FICO score.

Credit Score Impacts

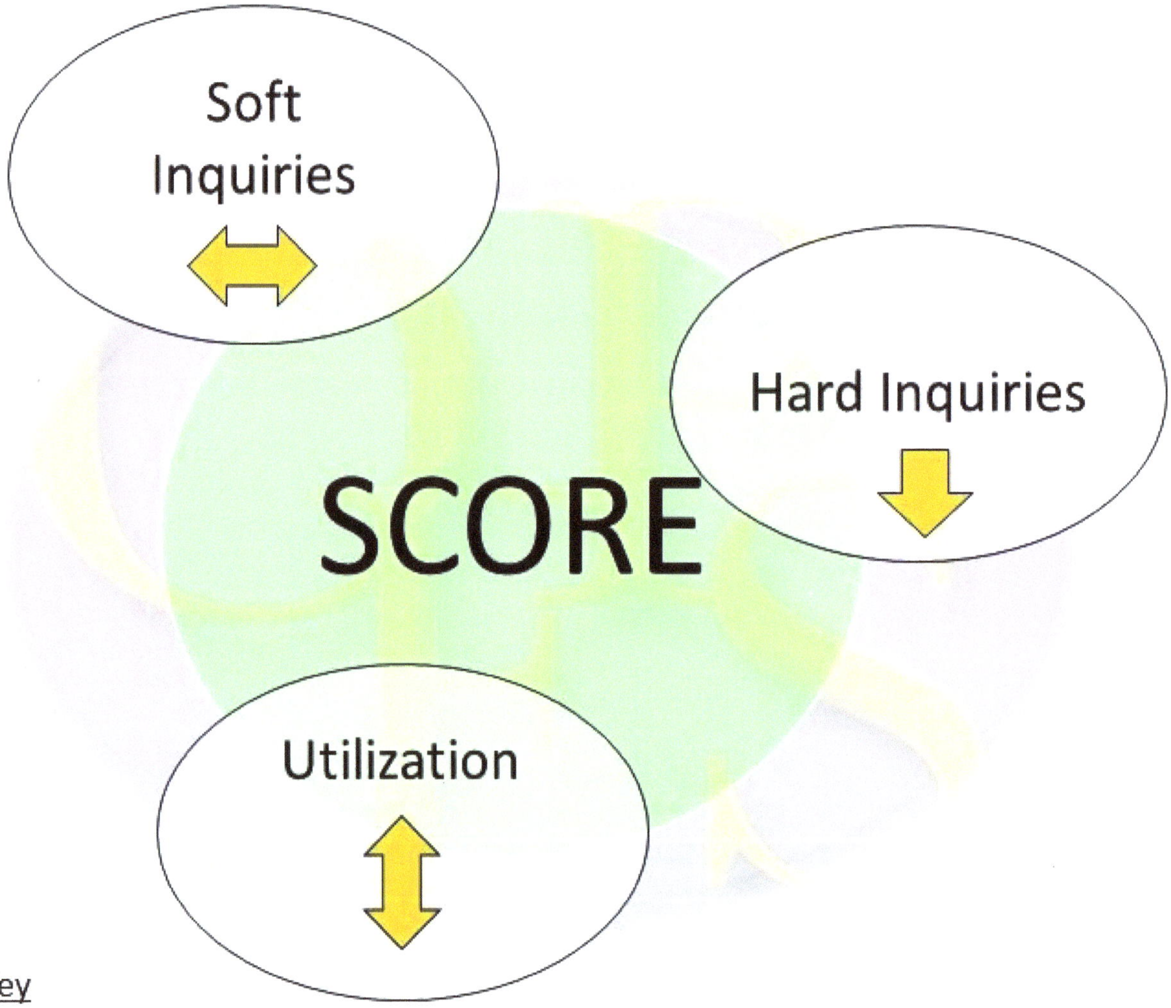

Soft Inquiries ⇔

Hard Inquiries ⇩

SCORE

Utilization ⇕

Key

Up or Down ⇕

No Impact ⇔

Down ⇩

Credit Score Impact continued…

I. Soft Inquiries: is when an individual credit is pulled when seeking employment, when an individual checks their own credit or pre-approvals for an offer. These inquiries do not impact your credit at all.

II. Hard Inquiries: is when an individual's credit is pulled when seeking to apply for credit accounts or loans. These inquiries can be a good indicator forasmuch credit seeking activity is kept at a minimum. Too many hard inquiries can negatively impact score.

III. Utilization: is an indicator of how much is owed on revolving credit accounts. This is one of the most important factors that impacts the credit score. A high ratio can reflect poorly on a person's credit score. The ratio will go up and down with payments and purchases. A good rule of thumb is to keep the ratio between 20 to 30 percent. Of course, lower the ratio the better.

Note: Mortgage payments usually have a major impact on credit score. Missing a payment could cause a tremendous drop in score.

Credit Utilization

Three Tips to Keep Utilization Low

- ✓ Making multiple revolving credit payments during one month. *(Note: Multiple payments may not avoid the next payment due for the following month. In other words, extra payments are not meant to be as paying it forward or used for a skip payment option. The next bill statement will be issued for the following month for payment amount due.)*
- ✓ Using revolving credit and spreading charges across multiple cards each month will avoid charging to or over the credit limit.
- ✓ Increase available credit if maintaining excellent credit and income has increased or little debt has been maintained.

Configure your utilization (divide the outstanding balance by the credit line and convert to percent) by completing the worksheet on the next page.

Extra worksheets have been provided.

Credit Utilization

NAME OF REVOLVING ACCOUNT	TOTAL BALANCE OWED	TOTAL CREDIT LINE	CONFIGURE UTILIZATON % (Balance/Credit Line)

A rule of thumb…keep the revolving utilization below 25%.

Credit Utilization

NAME OF REVOLVING ACCOUNT	TOTAL BALANCE OWED	TOTAL CREDIT LINE	CONFIGURE UTILIZATON % (Balance/Credit Line)

A rule of thumb…keep the revolving utilization below 25%.

Credit Utilization

NAME OF REVOLVING ACCOUNT	TOTAL BALANCE OWED	TOTAL CREDIT LINE	CONFIGURE UTILIZATON % (Balance/Credit Line)

A rule of thumb…keep the revolving utilization below 25%.

Credit Utilization

NAME OF REVOLVING ACCOUNT	TOTAL BALANCE OWED	TOTAL CREDIT LINE	CONFIGURE UTILIZATON % (Balance/Credit Line)

A rule of thumb…keep the revolving utilization below 25%.

Test Your Knowledge

Utilization: is an indicator of how much is owed on revolving credit accounts. This is one of the most important factors that impacts the credit score. Which of the following is a TRUE statement?

- ❑ A high ratio can reflect poorly on a person's credit score.
- ❑ The ratio will go up and down with payments and purchases.
- ❑ All the above.

Credit Tips

Six Tips to Improve Credit Score

- ✓ Check your credit reports at least every 12 months.
- ✓ Pay your bills on-time. *(Remember, when making an extra mortgage payment do not include with regular payment. Instead, issue a separate payment and apply ONLY to principal.)*
- ✓ Evaluate/lower your credit utilization to ensure it is below at least 30%.
- ✓ Do not close or delete old accounts reflecting positively on credit report.
- ✓ Don't apply for too much new credit. *(This will affect Debt to Income (DTI) ratio. Keep DTI ratio at least at 35% which includes recurring debt, mortgage, auto, credit cards, etc. A low Debt to Income ratio indicates sufficient income relative to debt and it is more attractive to lenders/creditors.)*
- ✓ Identify and change unhealthy credit behavior.

Credit Cards

DO'S and DON'TS

- DO NOT max out your credit cards.
- DO NOT charge over your credit limit. (*Caution; some credit card companies will allow you to go over your credit line.*)
- Avoid making the monthly minimum required payment.
- Request lower interest rate on your credit cards. Just because you were approved at an interest rate when you applied for card you do not have to remain at the initial rate.
- Keep your outstanding balances on your credit cards 20% - 30% of the credit limit. The lower the better.
- DO NOT pay all your credit cards to a zero balance.
- Stay away from too many department stores credit cards. They tend to carry high interest rates.
- It is a good idea to have 2 major credit cards and one department store credit card.
- Avoid credit cards with annual fees.
- Make credit cards work in your favor. Apply for cards that provide rewards and/or points to use toward airfare, hotels, products, gift cards etc.
- DO NOT use credit cards for cash you do not have.
- Pay regular monthly bills with major credit card if possible. In return use the cash payments that were going to be used to pay bills towards paying off credit card.

EQUIFAX, EXPERIAN, & TRANSUNION

All credit report companies contain basically the same information but may be in a different format.

- Knowing what's in your credit file is very important. Why? To avoid or correct any existing errors, mistakes and/or inaccuracies that can have a negative impact on your score.

- Request to get a copy of your Consumer Credit Report from all three nationwide credit reporting agencies. (*Note: A copy can be requested once every 12 months from each agency.*) Once received, review and verify all information is correct.

For more information on obtaining your free credit report visit www.annualcreditreport.com or call 1-877-322-8228. Deaf and hard of hearing consumers can access the TDD service by calling 7-1-1 and referring the Relay Operator to 1-800-821-7232.

Quick Reminders

Test Your Knowledge

You can receive a free copy of your credit report every 12 months or when you are declined for credit.

- ❑ True
- ❑ False

Sections of Credit Report

I. Identifying Information

II. Public Record Information

III. Credit History

IV. Inquires

Sections of Credit Report

I. Identifying Information

Includes your personal information such as your name, current and previous addresses, social security number, date of birth, etc.

II. Public Record Information

Contains information from local, state, and federal courts.

Sections of Credit Report

III. Credit History

Includes accounts creditors have turned over to any collection agency. Also, open and closed accounts are listed under this section.

Note: The credit history on a credit report is broken down in categories.

Sections of Credit Report

III. Credit History Categories

- Category 1 is where you will find the creditor who reported the information to your credit report. The creditor can be a department store, bank, hospital, auto finance company, credit card company, loan company, etc.
- Category 2 lists the account number reported by the creditor. It may list only a few digits of the account number to protect your privacy.
- Category 3 shows the responsible party of the reported credit account.

  (*"J" = Joint you and another person, "I"= Individual only yourself.*)
- Category 4 shows the date (*only month and year*) the credit account was opened.

Sections of Credit Report

III. Credit History Categories….cont'd

- Category 5 shows the date of the last payment or the date of the last activity on the account.
- Category 6 lists the type of credit account. (*"R"= Revolving example credit card, "I" = Installment example car loan.*)
- Category 7 shows the payment status of the account. (*This may include the type of account along with the payment status. For example R1 = revolving account that was paid on-time or paid as agreed.*)
- Category 8 shows the credit limit for revolving accounts or the maximum loan amount owed for installment accounts.

Sections of Credit Report

III. Credit History Categories….cont'd

- Category 9 shows the monthly payment amount for the credit account.
- Category 10 is the remaining balance owed as of the date reported.
- Category 11 shows past due amount, if any.
- Category 12 shows the date the credit account was reported.
- Category 13 indicates the number of times the credit account has been 30, 60, or 90+ days past due.
- Category 14 miscellaneous…..type of account (*auto loan, credit card, mortgage loan, etc.*), the status of the account (*closed, paid, or charged off, etc.*).

Sections of Credit Report

IV. Inquires

Inquiries are listing of the name of a credit grantor (*one who grants you credit*), who has accessed your credit report. Each inquiry is posted to the credit file so you will know who has pulled your credit report. "Promotional" inquires aka soft inquires (for *example; pre-approved credit card application*) do not impact your credit score.

Credit

Things to Remember

- Request a copy of your Consumer Credit Report once every 12 months from all three nationwide credit reporting agencies: EQUIFAX, EXPERIAN, & TRANSUNION.

- Once you receive your credit report use the credit report itemization worksheet to transfer information from your report to the worksheet to simplify and view at-a-glance.

- On the following sheet, credit report – aged accounts, configure the length of time an account has been on your report from the time the account was opened to the current date. (Use the Time Calculator Link to configure timeframe: https://www.timeanddate.com/date/timeduration.html)

For more information on obtaining your free credit report visit www.annualcreditreport.com or call 1-877-322-8228. Deaf and hard of hearing consumers can access the TDD service by calling 7-1-1 and referring the Relay Operator to 1-800-821-7232.

Extra sheets have been provided.

Credit Report Itemization

NAME OF CREDITOR	OUTSTANDING BALANCE	AMOUNT PAST DUE	CREDITOR PHONE#	CREDITOR ADDRESS	STATUS OF ACCOUNT
MEDICAL					
Total	**$**	**$**			
COLLECTIONS					
Total	**$**	**$**			

Credit Report Itemization
continued...

NAME OF CREDITOR	OUTSTANDING BALANCE	AMOUNT PAST DUE	CREDITOR PHONE#	CREDITOR ADDRESS	STATUS OF ACCOUNT
ACCOUNTS					
Total	**$**	**$**			
OTHER					
Total	**$**	**$**			
GRAND TOTAL	**$**	**$**			

Credit Report -Aged Accounts

ACCOUNT NUMBER	NAME OF CREDITOR	TYPE OF DEBT	AGED-ACCOUNT (Account Opened Date)	CONFIGURE TIMEFRAME (Divide Open Date Year from Current Date Year)	OPENED/CLOSED

Keep in mind, closing your oldest account could significantly reduce your credit score.

Credit Report Itemization

NAME OF CREDITOR	OUTSTANDING BALANCE	AMOUNT PAST DUE	CREDITOR PHONE#	CREDITOR ADDRESS	STATUS OF ACCOUNT
MEDICAL					
Total	**$**	**$**			
COLLECTIONS					
Total	**$**	**$**			

Credit Report Itemization
continued...

NAME OF CREDITOR	OUTSTANDING BALANCE	AMOUNT PAST DUE	CREDITOR PHONE#	CREDITOR ADDRESS	STATUS OF ACCOUNT
ACCOUNTS					
Total	**$**	**$**			
OTHER					
Total	**$**	**$**			
GRAND TOTAL	**$**	**$**			

Credit Report -Aged Accounts

ACCOUNT NUMBER	NAME OF CREDITOR	TYPE OF DEBT	AGED-ACCOUNT (Account Opened Date)	CONFIGURE TIMEFRAME (Divide Open Date Year from Current Date Year)	OPENED/CLOSED

Keep in mind, closing your oldest account could significantly reduce your credit score.

Test Your Knowledge

If you are a credit card holder, how much of the credit limit should be used to retain a good credit score? Select the BEST answer.

- ❑ The entire credit limit.
- ❑ Never spend no more than 50% of your credit card limit.
- ❑ Spend no more than 20%-30% of the total credit limit on any credit card.

BUDGET

"It is imperative to Set, Start and Stick to a Budget Plan."

-Stacey M. Oliver

Budget

How many of us maintain a **Budget** to keep track of our obligations and to ensure those obligations are paid timely. A **Budget Plan** is an excellent tool to keep track of all income and expenses. Look at it as an ongoing developing progress.

Be proactive in your planning. The decisions you make with your finances can be deliberated in advance. A lack of budgeting always leads to a lack of money. Remember, budgeting does not limit your income status nor your savings capacity. If you do not save or know where your money is going then you may want to take advantage of a **Budget** plan. Why? A **Budget** will keep you accountable and help you avoid spending outside your means.

Two key factors to budgeting are income and expenses. On the next pages you will find a break down and a variation of income and expenses. Review the terms and take a moment to fill in the appropriate blanks that apply to you.

The final page, **Budget Balance**, allows you to input and subtract the total amount of your expenses and income to determine if your final calculations (balance) are positive or negative number. Hint: You want your end total to always be positive.

Budget Income

Name	
ASSETS	
Income	
Rent Income	
Social Security	
Disability	
Interest Income	
Bonus Income	
Pension	
Dividends	
Other Income	
TOTAL INCOME	$

TERMS

- **Income**: take home pay; payments received for work rendered.
- **Rent Income**: payment received for use of property or land.
- **Social Security**: governmental system providing monetary assistance to individual with an inadequate or no income.
- **Disability**: monthly payments to disabled recipients.
- **Interest Income**: earnings/gains from stock, savings, certificate of deposits, etc.
- **Bonus Income**: extra incentive payments.
- **Pension**: a regular payment made during a person's retirement from an investment fund to which that person or their employer has contributed during their working life.
- **Dividends**: a sum of money paid regularly (typically quarterly) by a company to its shareholders out of its profits (or reserves).

Budget Expenses

Name	Monthly Payment	Qtrly/Annual Payment	Balance	Creditor(Payee)
EXPENSES				
Charitable Donations (Tithe)				
Savings Fund				
Emergency Fund				
College Fund				
Gifts Fund (Birthdays, Anniversaries, Just Because, Holidays, etc.)				
Vacation Fund				
Pay Yourself (Pocket Money)				
Home Mortgage				
2nd Home Mortgage (Equity Line)				
Auto Loan1				
Auto Loan2				
Credit Card 1				
Credit Card2				
Credit Card3				
Credit Card 4				
Loan1 (Installment)				
Loan 2 (Website/Domain)				
Loan3 (Line of Credit)				
Loan4 (Paypal)				
Student Loan				
Alimony / Child Support				
IRS				
Electricity				
Heating Fuel Oil or Natural Gas				
Water & Sewer				
Home Telephone				
Mobile Telephone				
Cable TV (DirecTV, Charter, etc.)				
TOTAL MONTHLY EXPENSES	$	$	$	

For more resources, please visit https://www.ofpsagency.com

Budget Expenses continued...

Name	Monthly Payment	Qtrly/Annual Payment	Balance	Creditor(Payee)
EXPENSES				
Auto Maintenance (Oil Change, Brakes, Tune-Up, Tires, Wash, etc.)				
Auto Insurance				
Auto Tax				
Health Insurance Paid directly (not by employer)				
Life Insurance Paid Directly (not by employer)				
Medical/Dental Expenses (Copays if not w/ER Flex Spending)				
Home Maintenance (Painting, Plumbing, Yard, etc.)				
Homeowner's Insurance (If not included w/Mortgage)				
Renter's Insurance				
Real Estate Tax (If not included w/ Mortgage)				
Land Tax/Lot Payment				
Retirement (If not w/Employer)				
Groceries (Toiletries, Personal Hygiene, etc.)				
Lunch Money(Work, School, etc.)				
School Supplies				
School Trips				
School Dues				
Transportation(Bus/Subway), Parking, Tolls				
Hair Maintenance				
Clothing, Shoes, etc				
Dry Cleaning/Laundry				
Internet Service				
Hobby (Supplies, Vendor Shows, etc.)				
Homeowner's Association Dues				
Recreation/Entertainment Money				
Gas (Automobile, Boat, Motorcycles, etc.)				
Other Expenses				
TOTAL MONTHLY EXPENSES	$	$	$	

For more resources, please visit https://www.ofpsagency.com

Budget Balance

- If the grand total is positive = NET GAIN
  Income outweighs Expenses

- If the grand total is negative = NET LOSS
  Expenses outweighs Income

Name:	
Total Expenses	$
Total Income	$
GRAND TOTAL (Net Gain/Loss)	$

INCOME – EXPENSES = NET GAIN/LOSS

Test Your Knowledge

To determine if your budget plan balances, the final calculations should be a _________________ number or equals _________________.

Fill in the blanks.

Hint: You want your final calculations (balance) to always be positive.

Getting Back on Track

- **Scenario 1**: During any financial hardships do not avoid your obligations. Contact your creditors to keep them inform of your situation and see if there is a hardship or work out program ideal for your circumstance or situation.

- **Scenario 2**: Bill rotation is helpful when budget plan is off-track. Bill rotation is when bills are rotated every 30 days until payments are brought current. Take two set-bills like auto and installment loan. Both payments are due around the same time but there is not enough money in the budget to pay each bill. Pay one on-time and the other bill before it becomes thirty days past due. *(Note: late fees may apply.)*

- **Scenario 3**: Do not avoid mortgage payments. Contact mortgage servicing company for options like forbearance, loan modification, refinancing, deferment, or repayment plan, etc. Missed mortgage payments have a significantly negative impact on credit score.

- **Scenario 4**: If an unforeseen crisis arises that causes a delay in timely payments consider paying the bills before the next payment is due until bills are back on track. For instance; if auto payment is due on the 5th of every month ensure the bill gets paid before the 5th of the following month so the bill will not be reported as 30 days or more delinquent. *(Note: late fees may apply.)*

Action Plan

Budget Plan From Scratch

Instructions to Start from Scratch

- On page 87, List all **set-bills** first and label as **SB**. Set-bills are debts that cannot be changed. In other words, if you do not pay these type of bills the results will be negatively reported and or placed in collections.
- Next list all **unset-bills** and label as **UB**. Unset-bills payment amounts fluctuate based upon usage. *(Unset-bills include water, electric, wireless internet, car taxes, etc.)*
- Then list all **other** expenditures such as entertainment, dining, etc. and label **O**. *(This category can be altered as necessary.)*
- As a result this will allow you to make as many adjustments as needed to create the right budget plan just for you.

Extra worksheets have been added.

Budget Plan From Scratch

BILLS	LABEL (SB/UB/OTHER)	COMMENTS

Budget Plan From Scratch

BILLS	LABEL (SB/UB/OTHER)	COMMENTS

Budget Plan From Scratch

BILLS	LABEL (SB/UB/OTHER)	COMMENTS

Budget Plan From Scratch

BILLS	LABEL (SB/UB/OTHER)	COMMENTS

Test Your Knowledge

Set-bills change whereas unset-bills do not change and other expenditures are not quite necessary in most cases.

- ❑ True
- ❑ False

Quick Reminders

Simple Budget Plan

A sample **Simple Budget Plan** has been provided for you to follow when establishing and completing your budget plan to see if you are spending more than you make.

Extra worksheets have been added for your use as you pay off debt.

Simple Budget Plan

MONTHLY BUDGET PLAN						
			ASSETS			
Income	$ 2,700.00 (Note: Gross Income $3,100.00)					
			EXPENSES			
Obligations	**Monthly Amount**	**BILL AMT TO PAY 1st pay period-15**	**BILL AMT TO PAY 2nd pay period-30/31**	**PAYDOWN/PAYOFF**	**DUE DATE**	**NOTES**
Tithe (10% of Gross Income)	310.00	155.00	155.00			*Due Each Pay Period*
Pay Yourself (3% of Net Income)	81.00	40.50	40.50			*Pay Each Pay Period*
Savings (3% of Net Income)	81.00	40.50	40.50			*Save Each Pay Period*
Mortgage/Rent	1080.00	1080.00			*15th*	
Home Association Dues						
Home Taxes/Insurance						
Duke Power	97.00		97.00		*30th*	
Water	53.00	53.00			*30th*	
Childcare						
Car Ins	77.00		77.00			
Car Payment	404.00		404.00	PAYOFF		
Car Taxes						
Gas	120.00	60.00	60.00			*Fuel Each Pay Period*
Wireless/Internet	76.00		76.00		*30th*	
Cell Phone	111.00		111.00		*30th*	
Family/Children Phone						
Food/Groceries	210.00	105.00	105.00			*Shop Each Pay Period*
Personal Hygiene Products						
Clothing						
Shoes						
Medical/Dental						
Cable						
Hair Barber						
Hair Salon						
Hair/Lashes						
Nail Spa						
Restaurants						
Entertainment						
Vacation						
Other						
Other						
Total Expenses	$ 2,700.00	$1,534.00	$1,166.00	Note: The red box totals should equal the white box total.		
Total Net Income/Loss (Income minus total Expenses)	$ 0					

*The easiest way to save is "AUTOSAVE"

OFPS

For more resources, please visit https://www.ofpsagency.com

Simple Budget Plan

MONTHLY BUDGET PLAN

ASSETS	
Income	$

EXPENSES

Obligations	Monthly Amount	BILL AMT TO PAY 1st pay period-15	BILL AMT TO PAY 2nd pay period-30/31	PAYDOWN/PAYOFF	DUE DATE	NOTES
Total Expenses	$	$	$	Note: The red box totals should equal the white box total.		
Total Net Income/Loss (Income minus total Expenses)	$					

Simple Budget Plan

MONTHLY BUDGET PLAN

		ASSETS				
Income	$					
		EXPENSES				
Obligations	Monthly Amount	BILL AMT TO PAY 1st pay period-15	BILL AMT TO PAY 2nd pay period-30/31	PAYDOWN/PAYOFF	DUE DATE	NOTES
Total Expenses	$	$	$	Note: The red box totals should equal the white box total.		
Total Net Income/Loss (Income minus total Expenses)	$					

For more resources, please visit https://www.ofpsagency.com

Simple Budget Plan

MONTHLY BUDGET PLAN

ASSETS

Income	$

EXPENSES

Obligations	Monthly Amount	BILL AMT TO PAY 1st pay period-15	BILL AMT TO PAY 2nd pay period-30/31	PAYDOWN/PAYOFF	DUE DATE	NOTES
Total Expenses	$	$	$	Note: The red box totals should equal the white box total.		
Total Net Income/Loss (Income minus total Expenses)	$					

For more resources, please visit https://www.ofpsagency.com

Budget Perimeter

It is important to keep your expenses at least 60% or less of your income (net pay/take home pay).

The other 40% is to be allocated as following:

10% = Contribution
10% = Pay Yourself
10% = Savings
10% = Emergency Fund

To determine if your expenses fall within or below the 60% perimeter use this simple equation:

Total Expenses ÷ Total Net Pay = %

Budget Plan Recommendations

Budget Control

- ✓ Open two separate accounts (checking).
  1) Bill Account
  2) Spending Account
- ✓ Set up auto-draft payments.
- ✓ Do <u>NOT</u> spend bill money for pleasure in hopes of paying it back later.
- ✓ Do <u>NOT</u> count your eggs before they hatch. In other words, Do <u>NOT</u> count your money before it's earned or received.
- ✓ Save extra funds/checks received unintentional or unexpected.
- ✓ Make plans to spend or buy.
- ✓ Avoid including bonuses and any other extra income within the budget for expenses.
- ✓ When planning a budget only consider your main income if possible.

Budget Plan Recommendations

Avoid Late Payments

- ✓ Utilize a calendar for on-time bill payments.
- ✓ Call lender to set up payment arrangements if unforeseen circumstance arises.
- ✓ Establish a new routine of paying bills.
- ✓ Call lender and request due date change.
- ✓ Make paying bills on-time top priority.
- ✓ Automate payments.
- ✓ Identify and change bad payment habits.
- ✓ Ask revolving creditors about hardship programs.

Action Plan

Savings

Jump Start

- Open savings account at separate bank from your regular checking account (for example; an online savings account).
- Save coins (piggy bank, empty containers/water bottles).
- Price shop comparison.
- Look for ways to save money (couponing, weekly ads, discounts, deals such as BOGO etc.).
- Do <u>NOT</u> grocery shop hungry.
- Make a shopping list.
- Shop off seasons.
- Know when to buy in bulk.

401K Investments

Things to Know

- When is 401k fully vested as of the participation starting date?
- Contribute to the MAX of the company's match contribution.
- Does the plan include a safe harbor investment option?
- What qualifies as a hardship withdrawal?
- Does the plan provide loan options?

ANSWER KEY

"Spending with <u>NO FOCUS</u> equals poverty."™
–Stacey M. Oliver

Answers-Test Your Knowledge

1.) Net Worth is an individual's total assets of what's owned minus total liabilities or expenses of what's owed.

- ☑ True Correct Answer
- ☐ False

2.) Utilization: is an indicator of how much is owed on revolving credit accounts. This is one of the most important factors that impacts the credit score. Which of the following is a TRUE statement?

- ☐ A high ratio can reflect poorly on a person's credit score.
- ☐ The ratio will go up and down with payments and purchases.
- ☑ All of the above. Correct Answer

3.) You can receive a free copy of your credit report every 12 months or when you are declined for credit.

- ☑ True Correct Answer
- ☐ False

Answers-Test Your Knowledge

4.) If you are a credit card holder, how much of the credit limit should be used to retain a good credit score? Select the BEST answer.

- ☐ The entire credit limit.
- ☐ Never spend no more than 50% of your credit card limit.
- ■ Spend no more than 20%-30% of the total credit limit on any credit card. Correct Answer

5.) To determine if your budget plan balances, the final results should be a _______________ number or equals _______________. Fill in the blanks.

Positive, Net Gain are the Correct Answers

6.) Set-bills change whereas unset-bills do not change and other expenditures are not quite necessary in most cases.

- ☐ True
- ■ False Correct Answer

DEBT COLLECTOR CALL LOG

"Financial Freedom is a Language"

–Stacey M. Oliver

Debt Collector Call Log

NAME OF DEBT COLLECTOR/COLLECTION	DATE	TIME	NOTES

For more resources, please visit https://www.ofpsagency.com

Debt Collector Call Log

NAME OF DEBT COLLECTOR/COLLECTION	DATE	TIME	NOTES

Debt Collector Call Log

NAME OF DEBT COLLECTOR/COLLECTION	DATE	TIME	NOTES

ACCOUNT LOG SHEET

"Unlock the door of your mind with the key of KNOWLEDGE." –Stacey M. Oliver

Account Log

	WEBSITE LINK	ACCOUNT#	*USERNAME*	*PASSWORD*
LOANS				
EXAMPLE: World Finance	https://www.loansbyworld.com/	987456321	JonDoe1	3JoN!Do3
CREDIT CARDS/LINE OF CREDIT				
UTILITIES				
AUTO INSURANCE				

Account Log

	WEBSITE LINK	ACCOUNT#	*USERNAME*	*PASSWORD*
LOANS				
CREDIT CARDS/LINE OF CREDIT				
UTILITIES				
AUTO INSURANCE				

Account Log continued...

	WEBSITE LINK	ACCOUNT#	*USERNAME*	*PASSWORD*
PERSONAL BANK ACCOUNTS				
BUSINESS BANK ACCOUNTS				
INVESTMENTS AND RETIREMENT				
LIFE INSURANCE				

Account Log

	WEBSITE LINK	ACCOUNT#	*USERNAME*	*PASSWORD*
LOANS				
CREDIT CARDS/LINE OF CREDIT				
UTILITIES				
AUTO INSURANCE				

Account Log *continued...*

	WEBSITE LINK	ACCOUNT#	*USERNAME*	*PASSWORD*
PERSONAL BANK ACCOUNTS				
BUSINESS BANK ACCOUNTS				
INVESTMENTS AND RETIREMENT				
LIFE INSURANCE				

OPFS

GLOSSARY
&
RESOURCES

Glossary

- **Assets**: valued property or item an individual owns free and clear.
- **Bonus Income**: extra incentive payments.
- **Budget**: map or plan of all monies expected to earn or receive and how it will be saved or spent: a way of goal setting or paying down or paying off debt: the amount of money that is available for, required for, or assigned to a particular purpose.
- **Credit**: no upfront payment for purchases based on the trust that payment will be made in the future: refer to one's spending/payment reputation status: the provision of money, goods, or services with the expectation of future payment.
- **Creditworthy**: financially sound and stabled to justify the extension of credit.
- **Credit Card**: open-end loans with a certain limit used by individuals to pay for everyday expenses/purchases or provide cash advances to be paid over a period of time which may incur interest on any outstanding loan balance.
- **Credit Report**: an individual's record of having borrowed and repaid money: payment history on recent and past obligations.

Glossary

- **Credit Score**: numbers created by mathematical formulas that use individuals' credit history to calculate their score.
- **Debt – to – Income (DTI) Ratio**: measures the amount of income a person generates in order to pay debt responsibly.
- **Disability**: monthly payments to disabled recipients.
- **Dividends**: a sum of money paid regularly (typically quarterly) by a company to its shareholders out of its profits (or reserves).
- **Expenses**: money spent to buy or pay for something; bill payments.
- **Income**: take-home pay: total receipt of money from work or service rendered, investments, etc.
- **Installment Loan**: typically for big ticket items such as home, vehicles, etc.
- **Interest Income**: earnings/gains from stock, savings, certificate of deposits, etc.
- **Liabilities**: money owed: outstanding balance for secured or unsecured loans and purchases bought on credit.
- **Minimum payment**: lowest dollar amount required to be paid each month on a loan, credit card, or other debt.

Glossary

- **Net Gain/Net Income**: the positive balance once the expenses have been subtracted from the income.
- **Net Loss**: the negative balance once the expenses have been subtracted from the income.
- **Net Worth**: assets minus liabilities.
- **Online banking**: managing your bank or credit union accounts through a secure website: bill paying method set up with a bank or credit union.
- **Pension**: a regular payment made during a person's retirement from an investment fund to which that person or their employer has contributed during their working life.
- **Rent Income**: payment received for use of property or land.
- **Revolving Credit**: commonly used for everyday purchases like food, gas, clothes, etc.: Accounts that do not require to pay outstanding balances in full.
- **Secured Loan**: loans in which property owned by individuals are used as collateral.
- **Social Security**: governmental system providing monetary assistance to individual with an inadequate or no income.
- **Unsecured Loan**: no property is used for collateral (most common type is credit cards).

Resources

Equifax

P.O. Box 74241

1150 Lake Hearn Drive

Suite 460

Atlanta, GA 30374

1-800-685-1111

Experian

701 Experian Parkway

P. O. Box 2002

Allen, TX 75013-0036

1-888-397-3742

TransUnion

Two Baldwin Place

P.O. Box 1000

Chester, PA 19022

1-800-888-4213

Resources *continued...*

Annual Credit Report Link:
https://www.annualcreditreport.com/index.action

Credit Cards:
https://www.creditcards.com/rewards-cards/

Equifax Link: www.equifax.com

Experian Link: www.experian.com

FICO Score Link: https://creditscorecard.com/

Identity Theft: https://www.identitytheft.gov/Assistant

Opt-Out Online Link: https://www.donotcall.gov/default.aspx

Reward Cards for Points (Compare Cards by Lending Tree): https://www.comparecards.com/reward?utm

Time Calculator Link:
https://www.timeanddate.com/date/timeduration.html

TransUnion Link: www.transunion.com

Comments

Calendar

MONTH ______________________________ **YEAR** ________________

Sunday	Monday	Tuesday	Wednesday	Thursday	Friday	Saturday

Calendar

MONTH ______________________				YEAR ____________		
Sunday	**Monday**	**Tuesday**	**Wednesday**	**Thursday**	**Friday**	**Saturday**

Calendar

MONTH ______________________________				YEAR ________________		
Sunday	**Monday**	**Tuesday**	**Wednesday**	**Thursday**	**Friday**	**Saturday**

Calendar

MONTH ______________________				YEAR ______________		
Sunday	Monday	Tuesday	Wednesday	Thursday	Friday	Saturday

Calendar

MONTH ______________________ **YEAR** ______________

Sunday	Monday	Tuesday	Wednesday	Thursday	Friday	Saturday

Calendar

MONTH ____________				YEAR ________		
Sunday	Monday	Tuesday	Wednesday	Thursday	Friday	Saturday

Calendar

MONTH ________________________				YEAR ______________		
Sunday	Monday	Tuesday	Wednesday	Thursday	Friday	Saturday

Calendar

MONTH ______________________ YEAR ____________						
Sunday	Monday	Tuesday	Wednesday	Thursday	Friday	Saturday

Calendar

MONTH ______________________________ **YEAR** ________________

Sunday	Monday	Tuesday	Wednesday	Thursday	Friday	Saturday

Calendar

MONTH ______________________				YEAR ____________		
Sunday	Monday	Tuesday	Wednesday	Thursday	Friday	Saturday

For more resources, please visit https://www.ofpsagency.com

Calendar

MONTH ______________________ **YEAR** ______________

Sunday	Monday	Tuesday	Wednesday	Thursday	Friday	Saturday

Calendar

MONTH ______________________				YEAR ______________		
Sunday	Monday	Tuesday	Wednesday	Thursday	Friday	Saturday

Take Action

TO DO LIST

Priority	Due Date	What	Who	In Progress	Done

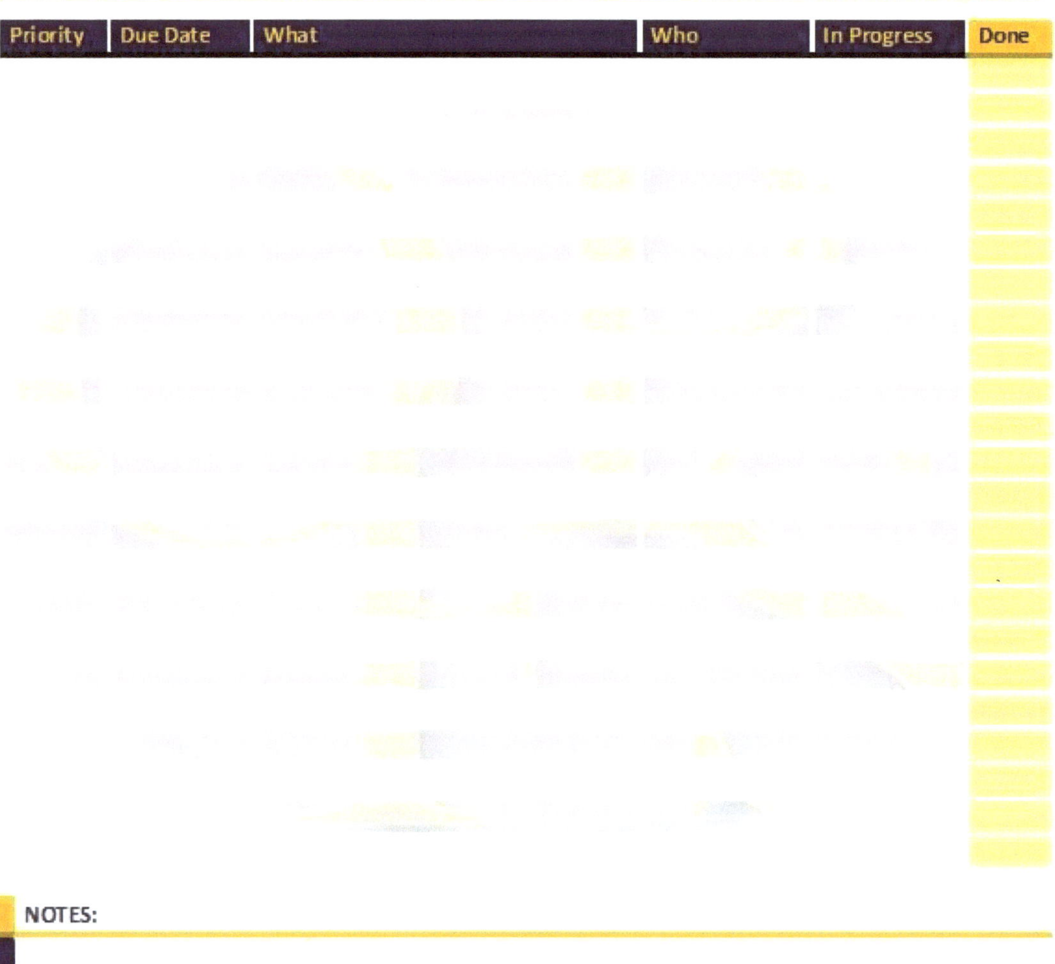

NOTES:

For more resources, please visit https://www.ofpsagency.com

Take Action

TO DO LIST

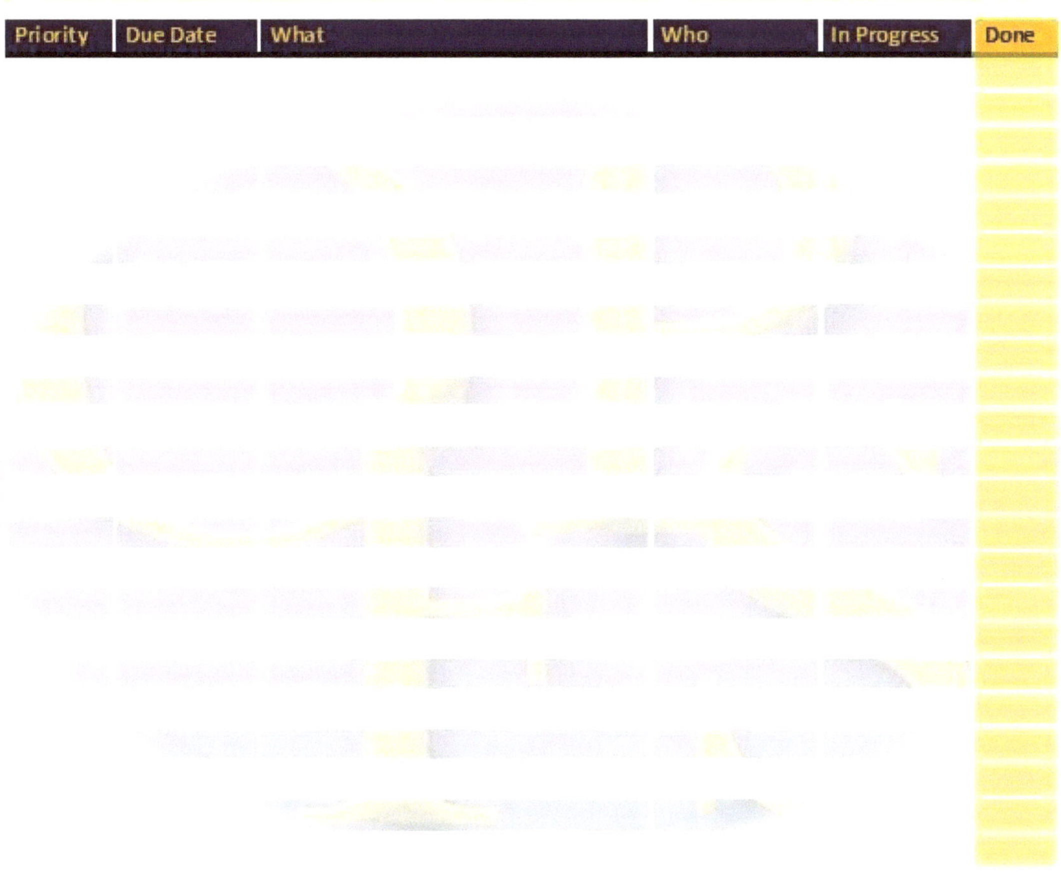

Priority	Due Date	What	Who	In Progress	Done

NOTES:

For more resources, please visit https://www.ofpsagency.com

Take Action

TO DO LIST

Priority	Due Date	What	Who	In Progress	Done

NOTES:

For more resources, please visit https://www.ofpsagency.com

Take Action

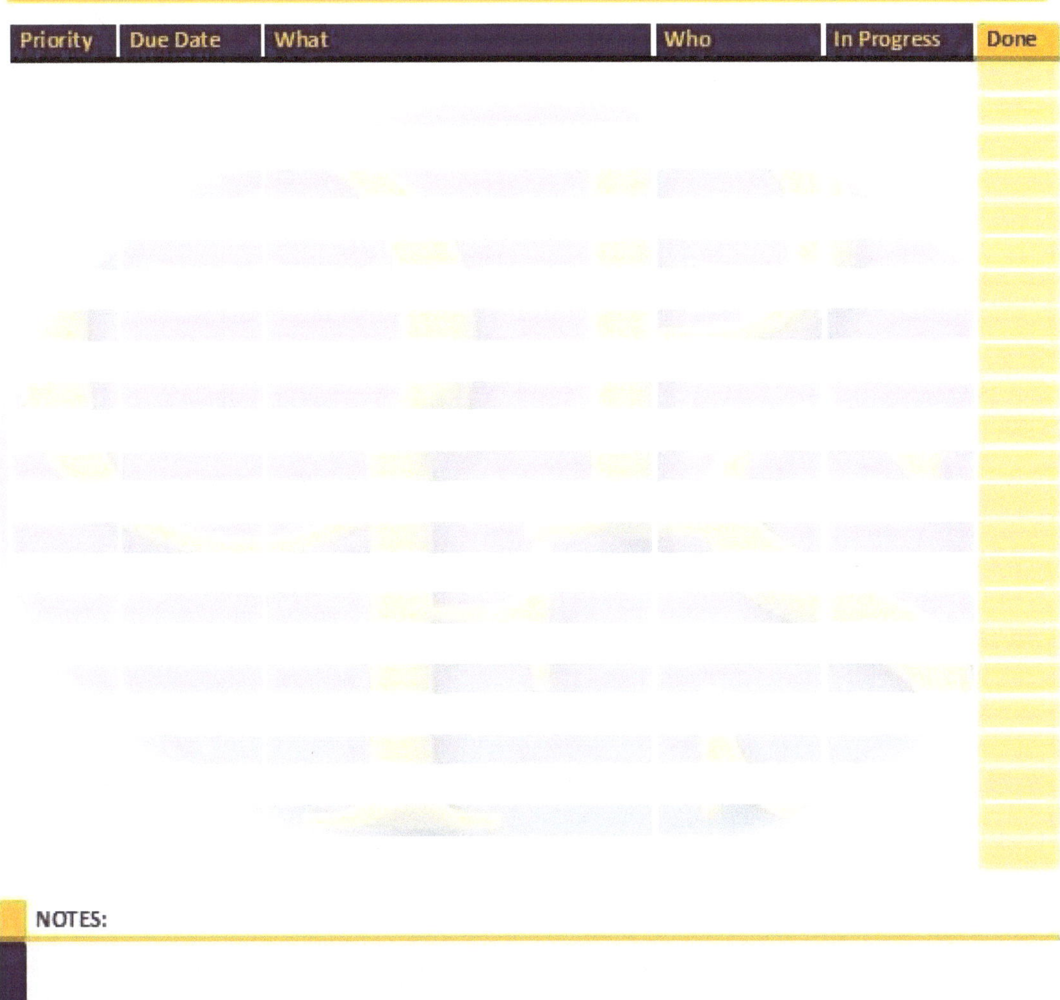

TO DO LIST

Priority	Due Date	What	Who	In Progress	Done

NOTES:

For more resources, please visit https://www.ofpsagency.com

Quick Reminders

Note From Author

Our Father wants you to prosper in excellent well being and great wealth. I decree as you begin to establish new divine financial habits and behaviors you will be blessed with such abundance there will be no room to receive it all.

Always remember, you are blessed to bless others. Your work will not be in vain, you will reap the harvest of your seed. As you align your finances to the principles and practical instructions from this workbook and God's word, you will discover your monetary standing altering and heading in the right direction to achieving total financial freedom.

Keep in mind, it is necessary to know YOURSELF, be focused and stay motivated by the ultimate end result- the PRIZE! – *Stacey M. Oliver*

Other Sources

Also by **Stacey M. Oliver**

The Master Key: The Master Key to Complete Financial Freedom

Complete Financial Freedom
(Audio Declarations)

The Master Key Financial JOURNAL

The Master Key BLUEPRINT Volumes
The Master Key Net Worth BLUEPRINT Vol. 1
The Master Key Credit BLUEPRINT Vol. 2
The Master Key Budget BLUEPRINT Vol. 3

Born to Win: Find Your Success
By Zig Ziglar

The Abundance Mind-Set
By Joel Osteen

Rich Dad Poor Dad: What the Rich Teach Their Kids About Money That the Poor and Middle Class Do Not!
By Robert T. Kiyosaki

Think and Grow Rich
By Napoleon Hill

Stay Connected

Olivers Financial Planning Services, LLC
(aka OFPS, LLC)

www.ofpsagency.com

https://instagram.com/oliversfps

http://www.twitter.com/Ofpsllc

http://www.facebook.com/Oliversfps

PO Box 51363
Piedmont, SC 29673
Email: ofpsagency@outlook.com

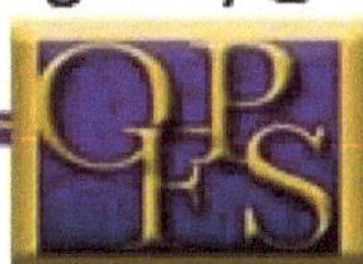

www.ingramcontent.com/pod-product-compliance
Lightning Source LLC
Chambersburg PA
CBHW041444210326
41599CB00004B/132

9781735092904